DAVE CLAYTON

REVIVAL STARTS HERE

A Short Coversation on
Prayer, Fasting, and Revival
for Beginners Like Me

A Discipleship•org Resource

Discipleship•org

CHAMPIONING JESUS-STYLE DISCIPLE MAKING

Discipleship•org

Join the Discipleship-First Community

We are disciples, church leaders, and disciple-making networks who seek to make disciples who make disciples. You will get an invitation to join our private Facebook Group, free disciple-making eBooks, and dozens of other great disciple-making resources, along with weekly updates.

First Name *

Email Address *

SUBMIT

Our Coalition of Disciple-Making Partners

Leading Voices · National Forums
eBooks and Print Books · Podcasts
Online Courses

"'EVEN NOW,' DECLARES THE LORD, 'RETURN TO ME WITH ALL OF YOUR HEART, WITH FASTING AND WEEPING AND MOURNING.' REND YOUR HEART AND NOT YOUR GARMENTS. RETURN TO THE LORD YOUR GOD FOR HE IS GRACIOUS AND COMPASSIONATE, SLOW TO ANGER AND ABOUNDING IN LOVE."
—JOEL 2:12-13

"IF MY PEOPLE, WHO ARE CALLED BY MY NAME, WILL HUMBLE THEMSELVES AND PRAY AND SEEK MY FACE AND TURN FROM THEIR WICKED WAYS, THEN I WILL HEAR FROM HEAVEN, AND I WILL FORGIVE THEIR SIN AND WILL HEAL THEIR LAND."
—2 CHRONICLES 7:14

CONTENTS

INTRODUCTION

Here We Go

Several years ago my wife, Sydney, and I began to notice the Holy Spirit gently and persistently inviting us to explore some deeper waters of life with God. This invitation from God came at what seemed to be an unusual time in our lives.

Just a few years earlier, we had launched a new church called Ethos Church with a small group of friends. By nearly all measures, things had gone better than we had even hoped. Not only was the church growing, it was multiplying, and we were having more fun than we thought was possible for such a challenging task. As the church rapidly grew, my family began to multiply, as well. Like clockwork, Sydney would give birth to a little boy every two years or so. Our three boys filled our house with joy, laughter, and even some chaos, as we learned to navigate these new seasons of life.

Life was wild and full.

We had a young, growing church.

We had an even younger, growing family.

Marriage was good. Parenting was good. Church was good.

Life was good.

And yet despite all of the joy, we had a deep yearning for more. We longed to see God move among us in the powerful ways we had only read about in Scripture and revival history. We wanted to experience this kind of life with God for ourselves.

It was during this crazy season that the gentle voice of the Spirit began calling us to push into deeper waters—to believe God for more. We began to realize that in many ways, despite our "success" in ministry, we were still like little kids playing on the deck of our father's sailboat as it was tied safely to the dock inside a peaceful harbor. Over time, we gained the courage to acknowledge that although it was fun to play on the sailboat, playing on the sailboat didn't mean we were sailing—and it certainly didn't mean we were sailors.

God began using this imagery of a boat, a harbor, and the open waters to illuminate what was a new way for us of understanding life in the kingdom. We discovered that if we weren't careful, we could become so comfortable in the safety of the harbor that we would never stop to ask whether or not we were actually sailing.

I believe it is possible—dare I say common—for many Christians to spend their entire life "believing in God" without ever attempting anything in life that actually requires them to exercise their faith. It is one thing to read stories about people who took great risks with God, but it's something entirely different to taste the sweetness of that kind of life on a personal level.

This temptation to play it safe, especially in the realm of faith, is still a real struggle for Sydney and me at times. Even though we have experienced the deep reward that comes on the other side of risk-taking faith, the gravitational pull toward comfort and certainty can still feel crippling.

Over the years, we have seen God move in astounding ways. Yet despite God's flawless track record, we still have moments in which we are slow to trust him, slow to launch out in faith again, and slow to set sail toward the open waters.

I don't know about you, but I want to be the kind of person who keeps pushing out toward the open waters with God.

I think I was made for that.

I think you were made for that.

And I believe that is precisely what Jesus came to offer.

It was that persistent call to explore the open waters of faith that led us to a moment God used to forever shift the trajectory of our life and our ministry.

God used the unexpected combination of:

a passing conversation

with a new friend halfway around the world

about an often-ignored spiritual discipline

… to ignite a desire to once again believe God for the impossible in our city and far beyond.

Let me try to explain.

SOMETIMES SEEING HELPS OUR BELIEVING

In February 2016, Sydney and I began a friendship with a couple named Muriithi and Carol Wanjau and their three amazing children. I could fill an entire book with stories about this incredible family, but for the sake of time and space, I'll share just one. The Wanjaus have been positioned by God in Nairobi, Kenya, and they lead one of the most amazing networks of churches I have ever seen. Our friendship with this family began that year when we got to spend several weeks with them and many of their global leaders who had gathered in Nairobi for a time of training and fellowship.

Sydney and I were blown away by what we saw during our time there with our Kenyan brothers and sisters. Their love for God, their passion for reaching the lost, and their commitment to living holy, counter-cultural lives were just a few of the things that blessed our hearts and challenged our thinking in ways we never expected. To top it off, the prayer life of our Kenyan brothers and sisters impacted me in a profound way.

One day, as Sydney and I were riding to the store with Carol, we were picking her brain about the spiritual vibrancy of their church network. We wanted to know why the Christians in their circle seemed to be so alive for Jesus. She was quick to remind us that there are no "silver bullets" when it comes to spiritual development, but she went on to share an important spiritual rhythm that has transformed their churches and community for the better. I will never forget what she said:

> "DAVE AND SYDNEY, MUCH OF WHAT YOU SEE HERE IS THE SIMPLE RESULT OF PRAYER AND FASTING. WE CONSISTENTLY PRACTICE THE COMMUNAL ACT OF SELF-DENIAL [FASTING] SO WE WILL HAVE THE STRENGTH AND CLARITY THAT IS NEEDED TO LIVE FAITHFULLY FOR JESUS IN A CULTURE THAT IS OBSESSED WITH SELF-GRATIFICATION."

That moment in the car with Carol is when many of the puzzle pieces began to click in our hearts. Little did we know that our family had arrived in Kenya on the last day of a month-long fast that the Wanjaus and their churches lean into every January. In fact, they spend nearly three months out of every year devoted to the Lord in prayer and fasting. Young and old, male and female, rich and poor, children and adults—all who are willing and able—commit themselves to a full-throttled pursuit of God above everything else through prayer and fasting.

The result of that devotion is inspiring to say the least.

I remember leaving Kenya thinking to myself, *If that is the kind of faith that prayer and fasting can help produce, then why have I given such little attention to this particular dimension of life with God?*

I'm convinced there are times when God will use someone else's life to ignite something wonderful and new inside us. Like a match in the hand of God, their life becomes the spark for igniting a new season of wonder and growth deep within us. I often thank God for

> If that is the kind of faith that prayer and fasting can help produce, then why have I given such little attention to this particular dimension of life with God?

our friends in Kenya and the way he used them to ignite a hunger for prayer and fasting in our family and church.

NOT AN ISOLATED EVENT

As I look back over the scope of Christian history, I realize that what we saw in Kenya was not an exception to the rule.

In fact, more often than not, it is the rule.

You would be hard-pressed to find any significant movement of God across human history that was not first preceded by a group of faithful men and women who were committed to the Lord in prayer and fasting.

I believe Jesus' words that those who "hunger and thirst for righteousness" will be filled.[1]

I also believe that most of us will never hunger and thirst for righteousness because we have been trained to feast on the junk food of our age. I wonder if it is even possible to truly hunger for Jesus if our souls are currently satisfied with far lesser things.

This is why I want to spend a few moments with you talking about prayer and fasting.

> *I believe your joy depends on it.*

> *I believe the joy of those around you depends on it.*

> *And ultimately, I believe the full revelation of God's glory in our churches and culture depends on it.*

In other words, I believe this really matters.

This conversation is not meant to be an all-encompassing discussion on prayer and fasting. In fact, for the sake of brevity, the bulk of my attention will focus on fasting because most of us are less familiar with this discipline. And since I believe you can pray without fasting but you certainly cannot do a biblical fast without praying, by default we will end up dealing with both.

I chose to call this book a "conversation" because that's what I pray this will become—not just between you and me, but more importantly, between you and the people in your life with whom you will sail toward the open waters.

As we embark on this journey, my prayer is that this conversation will help you move from *learning* to *living*. I hope it will help you to cut loose from the dock and set sail for the open water. If this discussion only leads you to think about praying and fasting, then it has failed. My prayer is that by the end of our time together, you will feel equipped and ready to take *your* next bold step toward God through prayer and fasting.

So without further ado, let's go.

CONVERSATION STARTERS

× Have you ever sensed God inviting you to know him more deeply? If so, what was that experience like?
× What has your experience with prayer been like? Do you find it easy and enjoyable to pray? Or do you find it more challenging and dry?
× Share about your experience (if any) with fasting. Is this something you have seen modeled? Or does it feel like a strange spiritual discipline to you?

TAKE TIME TO REFLECT

PART 1

WE NEED REVIVAL

Why This Matters Now

"HE ASKED ME, 'SON OF MAN, CAN THESE BONES LIVE?'"
—EZEKIEL 37:3

"WILL YOU NOT REVIVE US AGAIN, THAT YOUR PEOPLE MAY REJOICE IN YOU?"
—PSALM 85:6

"PRAYER IS THE VITAL BREATH OF THE CHRISTIAN; NOT THE THING THAT MAKES HIM ALIVE, BUT THE EVIDENCE THAT HE IS ALIVE."
—OSWALD CHAMBERS

Recently, a good friend asked me an important question:

> *"DAVE, WHAT HAS BROUGHT ABOUT YOUR SUDDEN PASSION FOR PRAYER AND FASTING?"*

It was a great question that caused me to do some real soul searching. As I examined my heart, I discovered that the answer was found not simply from our experiences in Kenya but maybe more significantly smack dab in the middle of a spiritual pressure point and a spiritual promise.

In other words, my soul searching revealed that half of my newfound urgency was connected to a **response** to the present, and the other half was connected to a **vision** for the future.

Let's start with my **response to the present**.

OUR CURRENT REALITY

Before our family left for Kenya in 2016, Sydney and I began to feel some deep spiritual angst. For anyone who knows us, this was a bit unusual for our dispositions. By every measure, we are optimistic, "the glass is half full" kind of people. During the season leading up to our global travels, however, we just could not shake the angst we were feeling. For a variety of reasons, we began to feel unsettled by what we were seeing on the landscape of both the American culture and the American church. By virtually all measures, most would say that both of these had seen better days.

AMERICAN CULTURE

In many ways, we began to notice that our culture was becoming increasingly divided and broken. Our country was drowning in the mire of racial tension, physical violence, political division, selfish ambition, sexual confusion, and spiritual disorientation. By all accounts, Americans had more money, more mobility, and more liberties than we had ever had—yet the fruit of "our excess" was proving to be rotten at best. In the midst of our so-called progress, our culture appeared to be "losing" in virtually every important sphere of human flourishing. But it wasn't just our culture that was suffering.

AMERICAN CHURCH

In many ways, the state of the American church was just as concerning to us. In his first letter to the Corinthian church, the apostle Paul told the church not to be so concerned when the world acts like the world. In fact, that is to be expected. He went on to say in that same letter, however, that we should be quite concerned when the church begins to act like the world.

I believe the church in America has lost much of her "saltiness" (to use Jesus' words from Matthew 5:13), and the results have been devastating. We have traded holiness for the pursuit of relevance only to discover that we have now been left with a version of "church" that is still unappealing to the culture but more significantly is also unpleasing to God.

> We should be quite concerned when the church begins to act like the world.

In large part, many self-professed Christians are living lives that look no different from the lives of their non-Christian friends, neighbors, and co-workers.

Millions of self-professed Christians rarely pray, rarely read their Bibles, rarely give of their resources, rarely serve the poor, rarely share their faith with the lost—and even worse, many seem to rarely care or even notice.

Many have baptized a form of humanism and deemed it Christianity only to discover that it is devoid of power and stripped of its godliness. We have attempted to turn prayer into a cosmic lasso in hopes we can wrangle the blessings of Heaven for the sake of securing pleasures on earth. In turn, we act like pouting children when God doesn't leverage the resources of Heaven to give us our fleshly desires. I believe God does want to fulfill us—but not like that.

In Matthew 7, Jesus warns that we will know a tree by its fruit.

Over the last several years, the fruit on the tree of American Christianity at large has often been less than desirable.

But the angst we were feeling was not simply a response to the present; our longing was also connected to a growing hope for the future.

IN MATTHEW 7, JESUS WARNS THAT WE WILL KNOW A TREE BY ITS FRUIT.

OUR FUTURE HOPE

Although our current reality has certainly driven us to our knees in prayer and fasting, it is the hope of God's future promises that has kept us there. The times may be uncertain, but God reminds us that our future is bright.

As followers of Jesus, we don't live under the cloud of uncertainty that plagues so many within our culture. The Bible is clear that the story of human history is working its way toward a beautiful and triumphant climax at the return of Jesus—a time in which men and women from every nation will gather to feast with God face-to-face in the new Heaven and the new Earth. It will be a time when the grace and power of King Jesus will eradicate all pain, suffering, sickness, and sin. I believe it is time for the people of God to begin living with a clear vision of the way our glorious story will end.

One of my favorite moments in the Bible comes from a passage in Ezekiel 47:1-12, which rarely gets much attention.

In his vision, the prophet Ezekiel sees a trickle of water spilling out from under the threshold of the temple. As Ezekiel follows the trickle of water running off of the temple steps, the water continues to get deeper and deeper. At first it is ankle deep. Then it is knee deep. Then it is waist deep, and then it is too deep to cross.

The vision ends with the trickle from the temple becoming a raging river that brings life and redemption to everything it touches.

Although the collective fruit of American Christianity is not all we would hope for in these days, I believe there is real promise on the horizon.

I sense the water bubbling up under the doorway of the temple in various places along the landscape of the American Church. And I don't know about you, but I want to see where the trickle of God's Spirit will lead us.

All across the country, I am encountering men and women who are desperately crying out for a fresh revival in our churches, in our culture, and far beyond. The words that A.W. Tozer wrote in the introduction to his book *The Pursuit of God* feel as relevant today as they did when they were first published in 1948:

> In this hour of all-but-universal darkness, one cheering gleam appears: within the fold of conservative Christianity there are to be found increasing numbers of persons whose religious lives are marked by a growing hunger after God Himself. They are eager for spiritual realities and will not be put off with words, nor will they be content with correct 'interpretations' of truth. They are athirst for God, and they will not be satisfied till they have drunk deep at the Fountain of Living Water.
>
> This is the only real harbinger of revival which I have been able to detect anywhere on the religious horizon. It may be the cloud the size of a man's hand for which a few saints here and there have been looking. It can result in a resurrection of life for many souls and a recapture of that radiant wonder which should accompany faith in Christ, that wonder which has all but fled the Church of God in our day.[2]

GETTING TO WHERE WE'RE MEANT TO BE

So the question remains: how do we get from where we are to where we were meant to be? How do we move from our current reality into God's future promises? In seasons like this, the words of Psalm 11:3 ring true in my heart, as David asks, "When the foundations are being destroyed, what are the righteous to do?"

As I listen to the words of David and look at the state of the church and culture, that question resonates deep within my heart.

> "IN TIMES LIKE THIS, WHAT ARE THE PEOPLE OF GOD TO DO?"

FASTING FOR REVIVAL

The longer I live in the tension of our moment in history and God's future promises, the more confident I become about the action God is inviting us to take.

> I've come to believe that prayer and fasting are **not only a way *but the way*** for the American church to faithfully step into the future with God.

In 2 Chronicles 7:14, God declares,

> *"IF MY PEOPLE, WHO ARE CALLED BY MY NAME, WILL HUMBLE THEMSELVES AND PRAY AND SEEK MY FACE AND TURN FROM THEIR WICKED WAYS, THEN I WILL HEAR FROM HEAVEN, AND I WILL FORGIVE THEIR SIN AND WILL HEAL THEIR LAND."*

I'm convinced that the future revival for which we were created is something we cannot acquire through strategic planning, relevant programs, or clever preaching alone. No, the revival we long for can only be acquired through sacrificial praying.

And not just the casual, half-hearted "pray when it's convenient" praying to which so many of us have grown accustomed.

This kind of future is only realized when the people of God become so collectively homesick for the kingdom of Heaven that we exchange our time, our comforts, our lives, and even our eating habits for more time in the presence of God.

That is why fasting is so important.

Fasting begins when the people of God acknowledge our current state of spiritual famine. It begins with admitting that there must be "more of God for people like us." The willingness to fast only emerges as we begin to honestly declare that our lives with God are not as they ought to be—and we refuse to settle for the status quo.

Fasting often starts with an acknowledgement of our spiritual famine, but it never ends there. Because *fasting is not ultimately about what we let go of but who we will let take hold of us.*

Fasting is not ultimately about what we let go of but who we will let take hold of us

Fasting is a physical declaration regarding a spiritual longing. It is a moment where we raise our white flag and surrender the notion that the fleeting pleasures of the world are an adequate substitute for the infinite goodness of God.

It is a declaration that what we really need is not of this world, and that we will not settle for less when God promises us immeasurably more.

Fasting is about our spiritual feasting, not just our bodily famine. It is about learning to trust the words of Jesus from John 6 when he declares, "Whoever comes to me will never go hungry." Or to trust his words in Matthew 4, when he says,

> "MAN CANNOT LIVE BY BREAD ALONE, BUT ON EVERY WORD THAT COMES FROM THE MOUTH OF GOD."

Fasting may begin with hunger pangs for what we gave up, but it often culminates with the deep satisfaction of what we've found—total satisfaction of body, mind, and spirit in Jesus himself.

I'm convinced that when the church begins to feast more fully with Jesus through prayer and fasting, the trickle from the temple will become the river that will redeem not only our neighborhoods but also the nations.

SO LET'S GO

I firmly believe God alone can transform a human heart and resurrect a spiritually dead culture back to life. But that doesn't mean we don't have a significant role to play.

I'm convinced every generation gets to choose just how deeply they will feast on the promises of God. Like the children of Israel standing on the

"MAN CANNOT LIVE BY BREAD ALONE, BUT ON EVERY WORD THAT COMES FROM THE MOUTH OF GOD."

edge of the Promised Land, we get to decide if we will live as though the Land of Promise is ours for the taking.

One generation heard the promise but shrank back in fear—forfeiting the deep joy God had in store for them and their children.

Another generation chose to push through the "perceived obstacles" to obtain all that God had in store for them.

I don't know about you, but I want to be part of a generation that pushes through.

I'm convinced there is more on the table for whoever will push through.

> *There is more for you.*

> *More for your church.*

> *More for our culture.*

But two questions remain:

FIRST, ARE YOU HUNGRY FOR MORE?

If you aren't hungry for more of God in your life, your church, and your culture—then the rest of this conversation probably isn't for you. Of course, you can keep reading, but if there is no hunger, the remaining sections will probably feel like a waste of time.

However, if you are hungry for more of God, I believe you will feel right at home as you continue to read.

SECOND, ARE YOU WILLING TO MAKE SACRIFICES FOR MORE?

This second question is just as important as the first. The school of life has taught us all that desire alone is never enough to experience the transformation we want. Nearly everyone I know wants to be in good physical health, but the desire to be healthy is not the same as actually being healthy. We must make sacrifices to obtain what we desire. The same is true regarding life with God.

So with that in mind, the remainder of this conversation will tackle the practical topics of prayer and fasting for revival (both personal and communal). I pray that you will find it helpful.

For now, let me leave you with the Words of God spoken through Moses as he looked out over a generation trying to decide whether or not they would step all the way into the promises of God for their generation. Deuteronomy 1:8 records:

> "SEE, I HAVE GIVEN YOU THE LAND, NOW GO IN AND TAKE POSSESSION OF IT..."

God had already given it, and yet they still had to take it. Isn't that an interesting reality? Jesus echoed the same sentiment when he said, "Ask and it will be given, seek and you will find, knock and the door will be open."[3]

In other words, the life you've always wanted is yours for the taking. But you have to knock. You have to ask. You have to take steps forward. There are times we must face the giants in the land.

Jesus taught us to ask God to make things on earth as they are in Heaven. What an audacious request! I'm convinced Jesus would never ask us to pray a prayer he doesn't intend on answering with a resounding "Yes!"

Just as the Israelites were invited to step into a land marked by the promises of God, I believe followers of Jesus are invited to partner with God in bringing the reign and rule of Heaven not only to our neighborhoods but also to the nations today.

To put it simply, I believe revival is what happens when God gets what God wants right here and now.

I believe a church and culture revived by the Spirit of God is the "Promised Land" God is inviting us to embrace.

Now we get to decide whether or not we will step into it.

I want all the "more" God has to offer. I don't know about you, but I think it would be fun if we stepped into this together.

CONVERSATION STARTERS

* × Where is God beginning to stir your heart for the people of your culture (i.e., your neighborhood, city, ethnic group, nation, etc.)?
* × What do you sense God might want to do in the culture around you?
* × What do you think revival would look like in your church or city or both practically speaking?

TAKE TIME TO REFLECT

PART 2

FROM BURDEN TO BLESSING

Recapturing a Biblical Vision for Fasting

"FASTING IS A PERFECT QUIETING OF ALL OUR IMPULSES, FLESHLY AND SPIRITUAL. FASTING IS NOT MEANT TO DRAG US DOWN, BUT TO STILL US. IT IS NOT MEANT TO DISTRACT US FROM THE REAL, BUT RATHER TO SILENCE US SO THAT WE CAN HEAR THINGS AS THEY MOST TRULY ARE."
—ST. THOMAS AQUINAS

As we get more practical regarding our conversation about biblical fasting, let's begin with a simple definition. In his book, *Fasting*, Pastor Jentezen Franklin writes,

> "STATED SIMPLY, BIBLICAL FASTING IS REFRAINING FROM FOOD FOR A SPIRITUAL PURPOSE."[4]

In other words, fasting involves our letting go of something in the physical realm to take hold of new things in the spiritual realm.

NOW THAT WE HAVE A SIMPLE DEFINITION, LET ME CONFESS SOMETHING TO YOU.

For the majority of my life, fasting might as well have been a synonym for "misery." In fact, the clarity of the above definition is why fasting seemed rather unappealing to me. I love food. More specifically, I love eating food. To be even clearer, I love eating good food with the people I love. The majority of my days are often scheduled around when I'm eating, where I'm eating, and with whom I am planning to eat. In our culture, eating is not just about surviving—it's about socializing. And so fasting didn't just feel like an assault on my survival instincts but maybe more significantly on my social instincts.

I would guess you can relate to that feeling on some level, as well.

There is a reason that American Christians devour books focused on dating, marriage, parenting, and finances but have to be persuaded to pick up a book on fasting. In fact, even finding a popular book on fasting is difficult.

I believe the reason is simple: most American Christians view fasting as a *burden*, not a *blessing*.

Fasting stands in bold opposition to everything we're conditioned to naturally do day in and day out. It feels unnatural at best and irrelevant and pointless at worst.

If you want to shrink a church or silence a small group, just try suggesting the idea of fasting together as a community. The only thing more awkward than talking about religion or politics is suggesting to a group of Americans that they need to take a break from eating food for the purpose of connecting more deeply with God. If most of us are honest, not only do we not understand fasting but also we don't *want* to understand it. The truth is if we don't desire to try something, then most of us will never bother trying to understand it.

This was how I thought about fasting for most of my life.

And yet despite all my reservations about fasting, the Bible seemed to be clear on the matter. Fasting is explicitly mentioned in Scripture more than seventy times, and it is mentioned implicitly even more.

Throughout the Scriptures, faithful followers of God would submit themselves to God through times of prayer and fasting. Consider just a few of these examples:

* Moses fasted for forty days before receiving the commands of God.[5]
* David fasted for seven days as he prayed for his sick son.[6]
* Ezra fasted as he mourned the sin of his community.[7]
* Esther fasted for the safety of her people.[8]
* Daniel fasted for twenty-one days as he sought clarity on a vision from God.[9]

The examples don't just stop with the faithful followers of God in the Old Testament. There are plenty of examples in the New Testament, as well. In the New Testament, we see:

* The apostle Paul fasted after his radical encounter with Jesus.[10]
* The leaders of the church in Antioch fasted before sending out missionaries.[11]
* In Acts 14, the churches in Galatia prayed and fasted as they prepared to appoint new leaders.[12]

But the most important example to me comes from Jesus' life and teachings. Jesus spent the first forty days of his rather short earthly ministry in prayer and fasting.[13] In one of his most famous sermons, he reminded his listeners that fasting was not something they *might do* but rather something they *will do*.[14] Jesus taught that fasting was not just a past reality but also a

IF FASTING
WAS SUCH A
BIG DEAL TO
GOD'S PEOPLE
AND TO GOD'S
SON, THEN
WHY WAS IT
NOT A BIGGER
DEAL TO ME?

future commitment for his followers[15] and that some demonic forces could only be dealt with through prayer and fasting.[16]

After spending some time in God's Word, I couldn't help but ask myself...

If fasting was such a big deal to God's people and to God's Son, then why was it not a bigger deal to me?

And so I began to wrestle with the role of fasting in my life as a disciple of Jesus.

REQUIREMENT OR REWARD?

I began to realize that if fasting was going to become a significant part of my walk with God, the first question I had to tackle was, "Is fasting about fulfilling a requirement or receiving a reward?"

To be clear, living into the requirements of God is a key aspect of life with Jesus. In fact, one of the most frequent messages of the Bible and Jesus' ministry is the message of obedience. Jesus clearly believed that our love for him is expressed most visibly in our willingness to obey his teachings.[17]

But as I studied Scripture, fasting seemed to be less about the requirement and more about the reward. Now before you write me off as a "health and wealth" heretic, listen to the words of Jesus himself from his most famous sermon—the Sermon on the Mount. In Matthew 6:16-18, Jesus says:

> "WHEN YOU FAST, DO NOT LOOK SOMBER AS THE HYPOCRITES DO, FOR THEY DISFIGURE THEIR FACES TO SHOW OTHERS THEY ARE FASTING. TRULY I TELL YOU, THEY HAVE RECEIVED THEIR REWARD IN FULL. BUT WHEN YOU FAST, PUT OIL ON YOUR HEAD AND WASH YOUR FACE, SO THAT IT WILL NOT BE OBVIOUS TO OTHERS THAT YOU ARE FASTING, BUT ONLY TO

> OUR FATHER, WHO IS UNSEEN; AND YOUR
> FATHER, WHO SEES WHAT IS DONE IN
> SECRET, WILL REWARD YOU."

I love this moment in Jesus' teaching ministry. To paraphrase his teaching, he essentially tells his listeners, "Hey, if you want the earthly reward of people thinking you are super spiritual, then just let them know you are fasting because people will always think you're spiritual if you fast. But if you want a reward far greater than a pat on the back, then commit yourself privately to God through prayer and fasting."

I believe Jesus knew that fasting is not about us somehow getting God's attention. Instead, fasting is about God getting all of our attention. And it is there, in the secret places of our lives where God has our undivided attention, that the reward of fasting comes to the surface of our lives in such beautiful ways.

JESUS WANTS THE BEST FOR YOU

One of my favorite moments from the life of Jesus is recorded in Mark 10. You might be familiar with the story. A rich young man is perplexed by the reality that despite possessing seemingly everything—something still seemed to be missing.

So he comes to Jesus, falls on his knees, and asks, "Good teacher, what must I do to inherit eternal life?"

And then comes one of my favorite sentences in the entire Bible:

> Jesus "looked at him and he loved him" (v. 21).

Oh, how I love that sentence!

Jesus looked at him. Think about that for a moment. What would it be like to look into the eyes of the one who spoke you into existence? To be face-to-face with the King of Glory? This is a stunning scene.

Jesus looked at him. He really saw him.

He understood him.

It didn't occur to me until just a few years ago that Jesus must have been roughly the same age as this young man. But it wasn't just their age they had in common. Jesus also knew what it was like to have everything at his fingertips. After all, before he was a traveling preacher, he was seated in heavenly places with all of the riches of creation at his disposal. And yet Jesus didn't hold on to his riches. He became poor so we might become rich in God.

> *Jesus also knew what it was like to have everything at his fingertips.*

Jesus understood this young ruler's dilemma. He knew he wasn't asking this man to do something that he himself had not already done.

But Jesus didn't just understand this man of affluence; **HE LOVED HIM.**

Jesus knew the path to life. He knew the pull of wealth. He knew the dead-end cycle in which this young guy was caught, and he knew that he had come to set this man and all of mankind free. Jesus was not trying to burden him; he was trying to bless him.

But the young man couldn't see it. For years, neither could I.

For the longest time, I would think to myself, *Man, Jesus, isn't that a bit much? Aren't you being a bit hard on the guy?* But the truth is that I couldn't see the blessing of a call to such reckless abandon—just the burden.

I am convinced this moment was not about what the young man was being asked to give up but more significantly about what Jesus was trying to give him. Jesus was offering him a front-row seat to the kingdom of God… a place in his inner circle. What an amazing offer!

> *Man, Jesus, isn't that a bit much? Aren't you being a bit hard on the guy?*

But instead, the rich young man left Jesus just as disappointed and unsatisfied as he had come to him. How sad: to be so close to having your life radically transformed by Jesus only to walk away and remain unchanged.

I've often thought of this story in recent years, trying to understand it more fully.

In the eyes of this rich young man, I've seen my own youthful misconceptions about the motivation of Jesus' invitation to life. I've thought about the many times I was convinced that the call of Jesus was more of a burden than a blessing. I confess there have been times when I thought Jesus was there to take instead of to give. But I now know that's not the heart of our Savior.

Now to be clear, following Jesus does come at a cost; obedience to the call of Christ can be difficult. But the motives of Jesus are always in your favor and for your good.

> *The motives of Jesus are always in your favor and for your good*

Let me speak more directly to you for a moment. He did not come into the world to take your joy but to give you the fullness of his. He knows you. He understands you. He loves you. He can be trusted with every part of your life.

So as we continue this conversation about prayer and fasting, remember that this is not ultimately a conversation about what you are letting go of; it is a conversation about what you are preparing to take hold of.

In the next section, we'll explore some of the barriers and breakthroughs you might experience as you attempt to let go of whatever might be holding you back from knowing Jesus more intimately.

CONVERSATION STARTERS

×   What is your natural disposition toward the call of God on your life? Do you tend to see God's call first as a blessing or a burden?
×   When you think about stepping into a time of prayer and fasting in particular, does it feel like a burden to be endured or a blessing to be received?

TAKE TIME TO REFLECT

_____

_____

_____

_____

_____

_____

_____

_____

_____

_____

_____

_____

_____

_____

PART 3

BARRIERS AND BREAKTHROUGHS

Learning to See the Whole Picture

*"THE PURPOSE OF FASTING IS TO LOOSEN
TO SOME DEGREE THE TIES THAT BIND US TO
THE WORLD OF MATERIAL THINGS AND OUR
SURROUNDINGS AS A WHOLE, IN ORDER THAT WE
MAY CONCENTRATE ALL OUR SPIRITUAL POWERS
UPON THE UNSEEN AND ETERNAL THINGS."*
—OLE HALLESBY

"SUBMIT YOURSELVES, THEN, TO GOD. RESIST THE DEVIL AND HE WILL FLEE FROM YOU. COME NEAR TO GOD AND HE WILL COME NEAR TO YOU. WASH YOUR HANDS, YOU SINNERS, AND PURIFY YOUR HEARTS, YOU DOUBLE MINDED. GRIEVE, MOURN, AND WAIL. CHANGE YOUR LAUGHTER TO MOURNING AND YOUR JOY TO GLOOM. HUMBLE YOURSELVES BEFORE THE LORD AND HE WILL LIFT YOU UP.

—JAMES, THE BROTHER OF JESUS (JAMES 4:7-10)

If we are going to make significant progress in our lives with God in the areas of prayer and fasting, it's important for us to have a clear view of both the potential barriers and breakthroughs that await us on the journey ahead.

If we can only see the potential breakthroughs, we will often be frustrated and disappointed by our inability to live into that which we desire. Like a person who has fallen short on their New Year's resolution year after year, we will feel like a failure if we don't first assess the potential challenges that stand between where we are and where we want to be with God.

As you have probably learned in nearly every area of your life, desire alone is rarely a strong enough motivator to bring you into your preferred future.

Similarly, if we only assess the barriers but never dream about the breakthroughs, we will not have the motivation needed to push past the initial discomfort. After all, it is a vision of what you desire to look like on your wedding day that motivates you to say no to that dessert or to say yes to waking up early to go to the gym in the months leading up to the big day.

The same is true in our walk with God. Unless we have a clear view of the breakthroughs, we will find ourselves merely learning about prayer and fasting but not living into the beautiful reality that this great discipline with God makes available to us.

So let's think about just a few of the barriers and breakthroughs we might experience as we attempt to connect with God through prayer and fasting.

SIX POTENTIAL BARRIERS TO FASTING

Although there are countless barriers that can come between you and your ability to humble yourself before the Lord in prayer and fasting, there are a handful of common barriers that I've often seen come up for those who are beginning this journey.

① DESIRE FOR SELF-SUFFICIENCY

The first barrier to biblical fasting is often our desire for self-sufficiency. Many of us have been trained from a young age to do whatever it takes to become self-sufficient. Our lives are marked by our ability to attain various levels of independence. In many ways, this desire can be God-honoring, but when this desire is not held in check, it can actually work against the very things we long to experience in God.

> *Our lives are marked by our ability to attain various levels of independence*

Although the Bible teaches us the importance of responsibility, it also teaches us that God has created us to be fully dependent upon him. Fasting will often confront many of the things you have been taught with regard to self-sufficiency. Fasting forces us to admit we are not self-sufficient; it reminds us that every fiber of our being needs God. Until we address the strong undercurrent of our desire to be self-sufficient, we will struggle mightily to submit ourselves to God through prayer and fasting.

② HUNGER FOR WORLDLY PLEASURES

Another barrier to a life of prayer and fasting is our hunger for worldly pleasures. If we have cultivated the taste buds of our hearts for the riches and pleasures of this world, then we will struggle to find value in fasting.

Fasting is designed to loosen our heart's grip on the temporary things of the world. Fasting helps us recalibrate the "palate" of our souls for the heavenly feast. Until we acknowledge that for which our souls truly hunger, we will struggle to see the need for fasting.

③ A BENT TOWARD SELF-GRATIFICATION

A third barrier to prayer and fasting is our constant pursuit of self-gratification. We live in a culture that bombards us with the message that *we can have what we want, when we want it, how we want it.* Fasting challenges this cultural narrative. Fasting is not about self-gratification but more importantly about self-denial. We are following a Savior who in Mark 8 reminds us that anyone who seeks to be his disciple must deny themselves and follow him.

④ HUMANISM

A fourth barrier is humanism. To state it simply, humanism believes that human beings are unquestionably good and their every need is of utmost importance. This ideology has crept into many Christian circles, slowly eroding our understanding of humanity's place in the created order of God. This pervasive thought leads many to believe that "we are a gift to God," as opposed to the other way around. Humanism is seen when our view of self is so high and our view of God is so low that we don't believe he is worth any effort or discipline. In this view, we don't see ourselves as sinners in need of God but rather as self-made people in need of a divine life coach.

When we succumb to this way of thinking, we immediately ignore any spiritual discipline that comes at a cost. In humanism, any spiritual discipline that reminds us of our need for God is seen as out-of-date and oppressive. Fasting, by its very nature, will often bring us into a deep awareness of both our sinfulness and God's holiness. Fasting has a way of resetting the cosmic order of our hearts. If we fail to recognize our tendency to embrace our culture's humanistic bent, we will miss out on many of the blessings that come through prayer and fasting.

⑤ UNDISCIPLINED LIVING

A fifth barrier is quite simply undisciplined living. I'm learning that discipline tends to breed discipline and lack of discipline tends to lead to less and less discipline. Often our failure to step into a life of prayer and fasting is not so much a reflection of our lack of desire but more typically a revelation of our lack of discipline. Embracing a life of fasting is not just about us battling the spiritual forces of good and evil but also about battling the practical forces of commitment and follow-through.

⑥ A LACK OF VISION

Finally, a sixth barrier between you and a more fulfilling life of prayer and fasting is a lack of biblical vision. The Bible tells us, "Where there is no revelation, people cast off restraint."[18] In other words, where there is no view of the breakthrough, there is no willingness to overcome the barriers. I believe this is the reason our experience in Kenya was so profound. It was the first time I was able to "see" that to which the Scriptures seem to so clearly point.

SEVEN POTENTIAL BREAKTHROUGHS
FROM FASTING

Recognizing that the barriers can keep us from stepping into a life of prayer and fasting is critical. But just as important is recognizing some of the areas of potential breakthrough.

To be clear, prayer and fasting are not formulaic endeavors. There is no guarantee that because we pray and fast we will experience the breakthrough we want. I do believe, however, that in prayer and fasting we will always experience the breakthrough *God* desires for us. So it's important to train ourselves to recognize the way God often works through seasons of prayer and fasting.

Let me describe a few results God consistently produces in connection with fasting, based on my experience.

① A DEEPER FRIENDSHIP WITH GOD (PSALM 42)

First and foremost, fasting helps us develop a deeper friendship with God. The ultimate aim of any spiritual discipline or practice must always be an increased friendship with God. We realize that God is never a means to an end; he is the end. As followers of Jesus, we pursue God passionately not because we think he is useful but rather because we think he is wonderful. We don't fast to make God do something for us or through us. We fast because we long to remove anything that might distract us from the unequaled pleasure of personally knowing and loving God. For example, look at King David. In Psalm 42, David plumbs the depths of his friendship with God in the midst of a fast—this is ultimately a picture of how fasting can bring us into the reward of God's presence.

(2) RENEWED HUNGER FOR HEAVENLY THINGS (JOHN 6:27)

A second potential breakthrough is an increased spiritual hunger for heavenly things. As I mentioned in our discussion on potential barriers, many of us have cultivated an appetite for the things of the world. Biblical fasting has a way of not only loosening our grip on the world but also, and maybe more significantly, loosening the world's grip on us. It is difficult to long for the things of Heaven when all of the things of earth keep us completely satisfied. As we empty our stomachs for a season, we often become more aware of the emptiness in our souls. As we begin to pay attention to the hunger pangs, the Lord often awakens us to the true hunger pangs of our hearts, as well. Here, in this space, we often begin to experience the rearranging of our spiritual appetites by God's gracious hand. As we enter into seasons of fasting, our heavenly Father will often recalibrate the taste buds of our hearts to crave eternal things.

> *As we empty our stomachs for a season, we often become more aware of the emptiness in our souls.*

(3) SOUL TRAINING FOR SELF-DENIAL (MARK 8:34)

A third potential breakthrough comes in the area of self-denial. In a world that constantly invites us to fulfill ourselves, Jesus invites us to deny ourselves. Fasting is one of the most helpful disciplines for training our souls to live into this pillar of discipleship. By saying no to the cravings of our bodies for a period of time, we train our souls to say yes to the apparently upside-down ways of the kingdom of God that Jesus invites us to embrace. Self-denial is not about being miserable for the sake of God but about making space for more of God. Self-denial is the natural response of our heart when we begin to believe that only Jesus knows what is truly best for us in this life and in the next. Fasting is a valuable practice for helping us step into this way of thinking and living.

④ INTIMACY, SECURITY, AND STRENGTH (LUKE 4:1-14)

A fourth potential breakthrough is often expressed in the connection between intimacy, security, and strength against temptation. Throughout the New Testament, the Scriptures surface a clear connection between intimacy with God, security in our identity, and the strength needed to live holy lives in the face of temptation. In the context of prayer and fasting in Luke 4, Jesus experienced intimacy with his Father, was secured in his identity as God's Son, and began to walk in strength and power over the temptations of the Enemy. Over the years, I have seen seasons of prayer and fasting strengthen and deliver believers from oppressive temptations as they've built intimacy and found security with God.

⑤ CLARITY IN PRAYER (DANIEL 10 AND ISAIAH 58)

A fifth potential breakthrough often comes by way of answered prayer. Just as Daniel received an answer from the Lord in a season of fasting in Daniel 10, we also can experience levels of refreshment and clarity in seasons of prayer and fasting. This is what Isaiah declares in Isaiah 58:6-9, as well. There are many times in which prayer and fasting will open our ears and our hearts more fully to God's answers to our prayers.

⑥ HUMILITY FOR REVIVAL (2 CHRONICLES 7:14)

A sixth potential breakthrough is an increased awareness of the need for humility—especially in connection with revival. Humility is a magnet for the presence of God, and fasting has a way of bringing us low. It raises our awareness of our sin and our deep need for God. Only when we have been humbled by our sin do we become desperate for God. Only when we are desperate for God are we suitable vessels for revival. Prayer and fasting often work to properly position us before God in such a way that God can trust us to handle his great calling on us, in us, and through us. I believe this is the reason you'd be hard-pressed to find any revival in human history that did not first start with a deep commitment to prayer and fasting.

⑦ FREEDOM FROM DEMONIC STRONGHOLDS (MARK 9:9)

Finally, many people will begin to experience freedom from demonic strongholds in the context of prayer and fasting. There is a beautiful moment in Mark 9, where the disciples struggle to understand why they cannot cast out a demon that has plagued the life of a young child. Remember, at this point Jesus has already given his disciples the authority to drive out demons. As a result, they are confused by their inability to live into the commands of Jesus in this moment. Jesus says, "This kind of demon only comes out by prayer and fasting." He says this to let them know that there are times when the spiritual battle requires the children of God to come into deeper fellowship with the Father before entering the battle. Prayer and fasting can often bring us into this place of spiritual breakthrough.

PREPARATION AND EXPECTATION

It is important to understand that preparation often reveals expectation. For example, when you spend the whole morning preparing a huge feast on Thanksgiving Day, your preparation reveals the expectation that there will soon be a hungry crowd ready to eat the feast you've prepared.

Your level of preparation reveals your expectation.

How you prepare for both the potential barriers and breakthroughs of a life of prayer and fasting will ultimately reveal what you expect to experience in the days ahead. You should expect to experience both resistance (barriers) and reward (breakthrough) in your journey of prayer and fasting. I hope you will prepare accordingly.

In the next part of our conversation, we will explore some practical ways to prepare well and expect much.

CONVERSATION STARTERS

× If you have fasted before, what barriers and breakthroughs did you experience? What things would you add to each of those lists?
× As you prepare to enter into a season of prayer and fasting, what barriers seem most relevant to your current season of life?
× What spiritual breakthroughs do you hope to experience?

TAKE TIME TO REFLECT

_____

_____

_____

_____

_____

_____

_____

_____

_____

_____

_____

_____

_____

_____

PART 4

READY. SET. GO.

From Learning It to Living It

"YOU DON'T HAVE TO BE GREAT TO START, BUT YOU DO HAVE TO START TO BE GREAT."
—ZIG ZIGLAR

"THEREFORE, EVERYONE WHO HEARS THESE WORDS OF MINE AND PUTS THEM INTO PRACTICE IS LIKE A WISE MAN..."
—JESUS, MATTHEW 7:24

As I mentioned in the beginning of our time together, the purpose of this conversation has been one thing—to help you take your next step into a deeper life of prayer and fasting.

For some of you, that will mean fasting for the very first time. For others, it will mean fasting with a new level of intensity and intentionality like never before. Regardless of where you are starting, my prayer is that you will be committed to taking a step forward.

Jesus made it clear in the Sermon on the Mount that information without application is not very helpful. Only when the words and realities of the Bible are applied to our lives will we begin to see the world of Scripture come to life in us. I am convinced that God longs to do more than any of us could ever ask or imagine, both in us and through us. But that sort of life will not come simply because we are more educated on the blessings of prayer and fasting.

> *We must actually take action if we want to experience these blessings.*

DESCRIPTION VS. PRESCRIPTION

As we begin to get really practical, it's important to note that these suggestions are simply that—my suggestions. Although the Bible often describes how people in the Bible would fast, it does not specifically prescribe how we as Jesus' followers should fast. Jesus deals with our motives, but he does not address the mechanics of fasting.

What I'm getting ready to share is not a prescription for how you should fast; it's simply a description of several things that could help you step into a season of prayer and fasting more faithfully and effectively.

Now, let's look at a few practical things.

FOUR PRIMARY WAYS TO FAST

Generally speaking, there are four common ways Christians choose to fast.

1. MAJOR FAST

A major fast is when you abstain from food or drink for twenty-four consecutive hours or more. A major fast requires a certain level of physical health, and it is recommended that you check with your doctor if you're doing a major fast that lasts more than a few days in a row. Some examples from Scripture of a major fast can be found in Matthew 4:2, Acts 9:9, and Esther 4:15-16, just to name a few.

2. MINOR FAST

In a minor fast, you choose to abstain from food for a certain period of time (i.e., 6 a.m. to 3 p.m. or sunup to sundown). This fast is sometimes called a "Jewish fast," and it can last for days at a time, eating only at a set time of the day. In a minor fast, most people will drink liquids during the day and have one small meal after sundown each evening.

3. PARTIAL FAST

A partial fast is when you give up only certain foods during the course of your fast. This fast is seen most clearly in Daniel 1, where Daniel abstains from certain foods out of devotion to God for a period of time. During a partial fast, some people choose to give up certain foods they enjoy in an effort to turn their hearts more deeply toward God.

4. SOUL FAST

Technically speaking, biblical fasting only refers to abstaining from food or drink (or both) for a spiritual purpose. However, some people choose to fast from things other than food. Some people will give up television, social media, or other activities for a soul fast to focus on prayer.

Each of these fasts can be a valuable way of connecting with God more deeply. If you are physically able, though, I would encourage you to prayerfully consider one of the first three fasts. There is something about giving up food that physically and spiritually realigns you in ways nothing else can.

SIX STEPS FOR GETTING STARTED

Now that we discussed various types of fasts, let's look at some practical suggestions for starting well.

1. SET YOUR OBJECTIVE

Begin by asking God to help you understand why you are fasting. For which of these reasons are you fasting?

- ☐ *Spiritual renewal*
- ☐ *Guidance from God*
- ☐ *Discernment in a certain area of life*
- ☐ *Physical healing*
- ☐ *Revival of the church*
- ☐ *Salvation of the lost*
- ☐ *All of the above*

As we humble ourselves in fasting and prayer before God, the Holy Spirit will often move us to pray for an awakening in our churches, healing in our land, and revival in our country and beyond. Allow the Lord to align your objectives with his objectives as you prepare to fast.

2. CHOOSE YOUR FAST

Second, you need to make a few decisions:

What kind of fast will you do?

- ☐ *Major Fast*
- ☐ *Minor Fast*
- ☐ *Partial Fast*
- ☐ *Soul Fast*

How long will you be fasting?

- ☐ *A partial day each week*
- ☐ *A full day each week*

☐ *Several consecutive days*
☐ *Several consecutive weeks*
☐ *Other:* _____

With whom will you fast?

☐ *Family / roommates*
☐ *House church / small group*
☐ *Friends*
☐ *Other*

3. PREPARE YOURSELF

Third, you need to give your mind, body, heart, and community the adequate time needed to prepare for your fast.

YOUR MIND

Prepare your mind. Fasting is just as much a mental exercise as it is physical. Begin asking the Lord to mentally prepare you for the journey you're about to take.

YOUR BODY

Prepare your body. No matter what kind of fast you're preparing for, it will require some adjustments for your body. I encourage you to drink plenty of water in the days leading up to your fast. It's also important to avoid the urge to overeat in the days leading up to your fast, which actually makes things more difficult once you begin your fast.

YOUR HEART

Prepare your heart. Remember, fasting is about your commitment to the Lord. I find it helpful to spend time in confession and repentance before entering a fast. I will often spend several days leading up to the fast asking God to forgive me of my sins, making sure I am in good standing with my brothers and sisters, and asking God to purify my motives as I enter into this time with him.

YOUR COMMUNITY

Prepare your community of family and friends. I have found this to be deeply important, especially if you have people in your family or household who will not be fasting with you. Remember, fasting is about taking a break from food, not from people. I've fasted many times without our children participating. It's important for me to prepare them for what we're doing so that it doesn't disrupt their lives. I want them to view fasting as a blessing from God—not a terrible thing their parents endure from time to time. This takes intentional preparation on our part. Growing up, I was blessed to watch my parents model this well in our home. Be sure to check out Appendix 2 at the back of this book, where I have explained what this sort of preparation looks like in our home today.

4. MAKE A PLAN

Fourth, you need to make a plan to use the times usually given to eating as times of prayer, worship, and Bible study. When our family fasts, we use this time to pray, worship, and read the Bible together. When I'm fasting but my family is not, I use our family meal times to share what God is doing in my heart as the rest of the family eats. Either way, making a plan for how you will repurpose your meal times is very important.

5. START IT AND STICK WITH IT

Fifth, quite simply you will need to start your fast and stick with it if you're going to make any progress in this discipline. Chances are, especially if this is your first fast, you might not make it as long as you had intended. That's okay. When you're hungry, pray. If you break down and give in to hunger, pray. Either way, get back up and keep moving forward toward God. Fasting is an exercise in grace—so make sure you give yourself some.

When our boys were learning to walk, there was a lot of walking, wobbling, and falling. Never once did we ridicule them for falling. We would cheer them on, help them up, and watch them go again. The same is true with the Lord and us. As we are learning to walk in new disciplines, the kindness of our Father is what lifts us up in both our struggles and our successes.

6. SHARE WITH OTHERS

Finally, share both the burden and the blessing of fasting with a small community. Keep in mind how the Bible is clear that fasting is not something we do for the attention of other people. So be careful not to let everyone around you know that you're fasting because that can allow pride to creep in. But you can fall off the other side of the boat here, too. That's why I believe it's important to fast in community. I have often found that my most successful fasts have been the ones I did with a small group of trusted believers. We were able to help one another push through the times of burden, and we were able to daily share in the blessings that come from pursuing God more deeply together.

Although these steps are certainly not a formula for fasting, I pray they will provide you with a helpful framework for taking your next bold step toward God in prayer and fasting.

In the final part of our conversation, we will explore why I believe your commitment to biblical prayer and fasting will play a key role in opening the door for God to do immeasurably more in you and through you for the sake of those around you!

CONVERSATION STARTERS

- ✕ What kind of fast are you preparing to do?
- ✕ When are you planning to start? For how long are you planning to fast?
- ✕ Is there something in particular you want to focus on during your time of prayer and fasting?
- ✕ Are you planning to fast with a community of people or by yourself?

TAKE TIME TO REFLECT

PART 5

REVIVAL STARTS HERE

Who's With Me?

"ALSO, SEEK THE PEACE AND PROSPERITY OF THE CITY TO WHICH I HAVE CARRIED YOU INTO EXILE. PRAY TO THE LORD FOR IT, BECAUSE IF IT PROSPERS, YOU TOO WILL PROSPER."

—JEREMIAH 29:7

began this conversation by sharing how this journey into prayer and fasting began for me, but I want to end this conversation by attempting to paint a picture of where I believe it's going—for us.

AN UNFORGETTABLE MORNING

Shortly after returning from our time in Kenya, we decided it was time for our church to get serious about prayer and fasting. Although we had led our church family through a few short periods of prayer and fasting (a day or two at a time, here and there), we had never led our church into an extended season of these disciplines.

> *We decided if we were going to do this, there was no need to tiptoe into the water; we might as well jump in headfirst!*

So we set aside an entire month, cancelled our normal Sunday worship gatherings across the various venues in our city where our church meets each Sunday, and called all of our people together for thirty days of prayer, fasting, and seeking the Lord together. During this time, each expression of our church came together each Sunday, all in one place, for a time of focused prayer and worship.

Although we have made our fair share of mistakes throughout this journey, during that month we learned a lot and saw God do some amazing things in us and through us. In the years since, we have continued to begin each year with a month-long fast, and we have seen God move in remarkable ways during these landmark seasons of prayer and fasting.

One such moment came for me personally, roughly halfway through one of these monthly fasts.

That morning, I had woken up early to pray, not because I am super spiritual but because we have three boys under the age of eight (and the only time in our house that's remotely quiet is in the early morning hours). As I was praying for my sons, I sensed the Lord asking me a simple question about my youngest son, Judah.

He said,

> *"DAVID, IF JUDAH WERE TO GO MISSING,
> WHAT WOULD YOU DO?"*

Even the thought of that nightmare made me begin to tear up.

I said, "Lord, you know what I would do. I would spend every waking hour looking for him until he was home safe and sound."

What happened next is hard to explain. I didn't hear an audible voice, but the word of the Lord came so clearly into my heart that it felt as though I had heard it with my ears.

I sensed the Lord saying,

> *"DAVID, YOUR CITY IS FILLED WITH MY
> MISSING CHILDREN. I WANT YOU TO WAKE
> UP THE SEARCH-AND-RESCUE TEAMS TO
> JOIN ME IN LOOKING FOR THEM."*

I'm not sure if you have ever had a moment like this—when you were convicted, inspired, overwhelmed, and everything in between, all at the same time. This was one of those moments for me. I sensed deep within my spirit that God was giving me an assignment to carry out, but I had no idea where to even begin. So I just sat with it for a few days.

A CLEAR CALL

Now to be clear, I wasn't trying to be slow in obeying, but the truth is I felt overwhelmed by what I was sensing. So I did the only thing I knew to do: I continued to pray. Over the next few days, as I reflected on these nudges from the Lord, another phrase began to roll across the landscape of my heart. Like a scrolling neon billboard, the phrase "Raise up an intercessor for every name, neighborhood, and nation represented in your city" started coursing through my heart and mind. But I thought to myself,

> *"HOW CAN I DO THIS LORD? I CAN'T EVEN RAISE UP AN ADEQUATE PRAYER TEAM FOR OUR CHURCH, MUCH LESS FOR THE ENTIRE CITY."*

But the Lord had made it clear to me. Even though he had not revealed all of the details, he had given me the direction. Our Father was not asking me to manage the outcomes; he was merely looking for my obedience. As if these nudges from the Spirit had not been enough, a few nights later I received all of the remaining confirmation I needed.

It was a Sunday night, and I was at our church's weekly prayer gathering. Every Sunday evening people from each of our churches across the city come together at the end of the day to seek God's heart in prayer about a wide variety of things. Toward the end of that week's prayer gathering, a friend came up to me and made a statement, cementing the assignment in my heart that God had begun revealing just a few days before. My friend Tom looked right at me and said,

> *Dave, I don't know why I am about to tell you this, but I sensed the Holy Spirit wanted me to tell you that it is possible for you to get a list that contains the names and addresses of every person in our city. I think you should get that list so our church can pray for them.*

I was stunned. Absolutely speechless. To this day, I'm still not sure how I responded to Tom in that moment. I bet I looked crazy and bewildered.

But just like that, the call became clear.

I knew the Lord was calling me to bring Christians together from across our city for a focused time of prayer and fasting, where we would collectively pray for every man, woman, and child living in our city *by name*. In the days and weeks that followed, the Lord began to make clear that this vision of a city-wide movement of prayer and fasting was bigger than I ever imagined. Although this vision would start in our city, it certainly would not end there.

AN IMPOSSIBLE TASK?

I have to admit, the vision felt overwhelming on all fronts.

However, once I obtained the list of the names of every person in our city, the vision went from feeling overwhelming to feeling downright impossible.

The sheer size of our city, along with my newly obtained list and the corresponding logistics of praying for that many people, honestly made me want to quit before we even started.

> Wow, this sounds amazing but....

Nearly every person with whom I shared the vision during those first few months had a pretty similar response. They would say things like, "Wow, this sounds amazing but…"

- × *"Don't you know that churches in our city don't really play well together?"*
- × *"Don't you know that Americans aren't really into fasting?"*
- × *"Don't you know that Americans are too busy and distracted to pray for an entire month?"*

The list went on and on. Each time, it was a slightly different response but the same underlying message:

"DAVE, THIS WILL NEVER WORK."

But with every discouraging word of advice, I was reminded that God was not asking me to manage the outcomes or even people's expectations; he was simply asking me to trust him.

REASON TO BELIEVE

Amidst all of the discouragement, a spirit of unshakeable faith began to rise up deep within me. Was the vision big? Absolutely. And it should be if it's from God! We worship a God who specializes in the impossible.

I don't know about you, but I'm tired of pursuing things that can be accomplished without any help from the living God.

> But my reason for belief was not merely sentimental.

Instead, my belief was anchored in the **promises of Scripture**. God declares in 2 Chronicles 7:14: "If my people, who are called by my name, will humble themselves and pray and seek my face and turn from their wicked ways, then I will hear from heaven, and I will forgive their sin and will heal their land." Scripture promises that God will respond to repentant, humble hearts!

But it wasn't just the promises of Scripture that gave me confidence; it was also the **proof of history**. Entire books have been written on this one point alone. As I said earlier, you would be hard-pressed to find a single revival in human history that was not first preceded by a movement of prayer and fasting. But despite all of our knowledge of this reality, there is very little commitment to this discipline.

Beyond the promises of Scripture and the proof of history was also the **prevailing need of our day**. As I mentioned before, both the American church and culture have seen better days. But any student of the Scriptures knows that the darker the cultural moment, the brighter the opportunity for the light of the gospel to shine. I believe we are long overdue for a fresh touch from God, and our current moment in history stands as a wonderful backdrop for the beauty of Christ to be seen.

Finally, my faith continued to swell as I reflected on **the power of God** to change even the most impossible of situations. C.S. Lewis famously said that prayer doesn't just change things; it changes us. I believe that's absolutely true. But let me go on the record saying that I don't just pray for my transformation alone; I pray because I believe I am communicating with the God who parted the Red Sea, the God who calmed the storms of Galilee, who miraculously fed the five thousand, and who raised Jesus to life! I pray to the one who is *willing and able* to bring about change in ways I could never dream or imagine. That is why I pray.

And that is why I am calling the churches of our city and beyond to pray and fast for the sake of God's lost kids. I am praying that God will use our prayers to bring many of his children home!

WHAT IS GOING TO HAPPEN?

As I've been sharing this vision in recent months, one of the questions I have been repeatedly asked is, "How will we know if this worked?"

First, I think as Americans we need to be cautious of how we measure success. Outcomes in the kingdom of God rarely align with our understanding of success, which tends to significantly differ from God's.

But with that being said, I believe there will be plenty to see as we humble ourselves in prayer and fasting. Allow me to be specific:

Just like the revivals of old that have swept through our country in centuries past, I believe we will see a spirit of repentance grip the hearts of our church and culture. Men and women, young and old, will begin to take seriously the sins that have kept them far from God.

I believe we will see the fear of the Lord once again established as a pillar within our churches.

I believe we will see a spirit of genuine joy in worship, unity in fellowship, and passion for prayer return to the body of Christ in ways that don't have to be programmatically implemented or coerced.

I believe we will see marriages restored, children and parents reconnected, and the fruit of the Spirit flourish in our lives both personally and communally.

I believe we will see the church filled with the Spirit of God in such a mighty way that our love for God and our love for neighbor will only be accurately described as a "supernatural impartation of love."

I believe we will see people from every nation and race coming together under the name of Jesus in an unprecedented wave of unity.

I believe we will see men and women mobilized by the Spirit of God to effectively bless and reach the culture around them.

I believe the words of John 14:12 will become true in our midst—that we will see the church doing "even greater things" just as Jesus said we would!

AND THAT IS JUST IN THE CHURCH!

I believe we will also see a great outpouring of God's Spirit into the culture, as well:

People from every walk of life will become more receptive to the Good News of Jesus.

Addictions and spiritual strongholds will be broken.

Violent crimes will decrease dramatically.

The fruit of hell (anger, bitterness, envy, greed, lust, pride, etc.) will begin to diminish.

The sick will be healed, and the spiritually dead will be raised to life in Christ.

Will everything be perfect? Of course not! Perfection will only be tasted in the future kingdom of Heaven, but I do believe we will have no doubt as to whether or not we are experiencing true revival. There will be plenty to see!

But for everything we do see, I am convinced there will be so much more that we never see—or understand. And this is where our faith is developed.

Just as the church in ancient Antioch had no idea their commitment to prayer and fasting in Acts 13 would unleash the greatest missionary the world would ever see (Paul), I believe our commitment to pray and fast will shift the spiritual trajectory of future generations in ways we are incapable of understanding from our limited perspective.

One of the many beautiful aspects of prayer is that it always outlives the one who prayed it. We see this throughout Scripture. One generation often receives God's gracious answer to the previous generation's prayers. In fact,

I guarantee you that you have been the recipient of God's gracious answer to someone else's prayers.

What will happen as hundreds of churches and tens of thousands of Christians from all across our city come together for an intentional time of prayer and fasting for the people of our city? What will happen around our nation, if thousands of churches and hundreds of thousands of Christians pray and fast together for the sake of nationwide revival? Truthfully, I don't know exactly what will come of it. But I also know we won't know unless we try.

Whatever God has in store (although it might look different than we expected) will be immeasurably better than we could ever imagine. I am deeply convinced that God is going to use a unified group of churches to shift the spiritual foundation of an entire generation. And I believe this shift will start as we come together in prayer and fasting.

Let's Join Together

So will you join me? Will you untie your boats, push away from the dock, and head toward the open waters?

Will you join me in prayer for the church, our nation, and our world?

Will you join me as we humble ourselves before God on behalf of the sins of the church and our culture?

Will you join me in praying that God would tear open Heaven and pour out his presence on the church and the culture?

Will you join me in praying that God will raise up workers for the spiritual harvest?

Will you join me in believing that our heavenly Father is exceedingly good and that he longs to do more than we could ever ask or imagine if only we would come to him with humble hearts according to his terms and the grace of Jesus Christ?

But first we must believe. In the often-quoted words of South African revivalist Andrew Murray,

> "WE MUST BEGIN TO BELIEVE THAT GOD,
> IN THE MYSTERY OF PRAYER AND FASTING,
> HAS ENTRUSTED US WITH A FORCE THAT
> CAN MOVE THE HEAVENLY WORLD, AND
> BRING ITS POWER DOWN TO EARTH."

So, enough with the talking. It's time to start.

It's time to start fasting and praying—for God's glory, our joy, and the good of all people.

Who's with me?

Father,

You know the heart of my brothers and sisters reading this book. You know the challenges they are facing and the dreams they are dreaming. Holy Spirit, will you be their gracious teacher? Will you take my brothers and sisters by the hand and lead them every step of the way as they try to know you more deeply in prayer and fasting? Will you empower them to lead their churches to pursue you more deeply? Will you bring about a disproportionate amount of spiritual fruit in their life, their church, and their city for your glory, their joy, and the good of the people in their city?

In the perfect name of Jesus,

Amen

DISCUSSION STARTERS

× Name three people you love who aren't yet followers of Jesus. Will you commit to praying for them daily until they become disciples of Jesus?

× Where do you sense God wants to revive you or your family or both? Write down a few specific ways you are hoping God will bring about transformation and then spend time praying toward that goal.

× Where do you believe your church needs a fresh awakening? Humbly ask God to awaken any part of your local church that is "spiritually sleepy" or dead.

× Spend some time asking God to give you insight into how he would have you pray for your city. Once you have clarity, will you commit to praying for your city each day?

TAKE TIME TO REFLECT

ENDNOTES

1. Matthew 5:6.
2. From the first page of the preface of A. W. Tozer's *The Pursuit of God*, which was originally published in 1948 by Christian Publications, Inc., updated in 2015.
3. Matthew 7:7.
4. Published by Charisma House in 2008. The definition of fasting comes from page 9.
5. Deuteronomy 9:9-18.
6. 2 Samuel 12:16.
7. Ezra 10:6.
8. Esther 4:15-17.
9. Daniel 10:1-3.
10. Acts 9:9.
11. Acts 13:2.
12. Acts 14:21-23.
13. Matthew 4:1-11.
14. Matthew 6:16-18.
15. Luke 5:35.
16. Mark 9:29.
17. John 14:15.
18. Proverbs 29:18.

PRACTICAL
IDEAS

.

Applying What You've Learned

A DAY OF FASTING

Practical Ideas

A common question for many people as they fast for the first time is, "Besides abstaining from food, what else should I do during the day (or days) that I fast?" Below are a few suggestions that might help you connect more deeply with God as you pray and fast.

SUGGESTIONS FOR MORNING

I have found that the way I begin my day will often set the tone for the rest of it. This is especially true during seasons of fasting. I encourage you to:

- × Begin your day in praise and worship.
- × Read and meditate on God's Word.
- × Invite the Holy Spirit to search your heart and life.
- × Invite God to use you to influence your family, workplace, neighborhood, and world.
- × Ask God to give you his vision for your life.
- × Ask God to empower you to do his will.

MIDDAY SUGGESTIONS

Another significant time of day is the lunch hour. With a little bit of intentionality, this can become something you look forward to (and not merely survive) during your fast. I encourage you to dedicate your lunchtime to the Lord by:

* Returning to God in prayer and Scripture.
* Taking a short prayer walk.
* Spending a few moments in silence reflecting on God's goodness.
* Use your lunch hour to meet up with others with whom you are fasting to pray, worship, and set your hearts on God together.

EVENING SUGGESTIONS

Finally, the way you end your day will set the tone for the next one. In the Old Testament, each day began around dinnertime. The Hebrew people viewed the evening as a time of preparation for the hours ahead. With that in mind, I encourage you to:

* Spend some unhurried time with God without the pressures or constraints of work or school.
* Meet up or video chat with others who are fasting for a time of prayer and encouragement.
* Avoid or limit outside distractions such as television or social media.
* Spend some time on your knees in prayer with your spouse, children, or roommates.

FASTING WITH YOUR KIDS

How to Lead Your Family During a Fast

F asting can be an incredible way to experience God's presence in the life of your family. During our time in Kenya, we were blown away by how entire families would devote themselves to God through prayer and fasting. Since then, our family has experienced successes and challenges when fasting with our three young boys. Below are a few things you might find helpful when fasting with your kids.

START BY TALKING ABOUT IT

Explain to your kids what fasting is, why you are doing it, and for how long you'll be doing it.

We found mealtimes to be easy opportunities to share what God was doing in our hearts because our kids noticed we were not eating.

Share the blessings you're experiencing and not simply the burdens you might be feeling.

PREPARE AHEAD

One of the most challenging aspects of fasting as a family is that often the parents must still prepare meals for the kids who are eating.

Share the blessings you're experiencing and not simply the burdens you might be feeling.

You can eliminate some of the struggle of food prep by planning ahead, or at the very least sharing the load as a couple to avoid both the temptation of eating and the time constraints that come with preparing a meal for others.

INVITE THEM IN

Invite your kids to pray about whether or not they would like to fast with you.

We have discovered that when our kids see us fasting and hear about the blessings we are experiencing with the Lord, they will often ask to join us in the fast.

When we're doing an extended fast, due to the age of our kids, we only allow them to fast from one meal, no more than one day per week. This gives them the ability to participate with us in a healthy way.

START SMALL

If your kids want to join you, have them commit to fasting from one meal or snack as a starting point.

CHANGE THE SCENERY

When your kids are fasting with you, get out of the house during meal times. Go for a walk. Play at the park. Pray for your friends and family members. Whatever you do, try to change the setting during key mealtimes. It will be especially helpful for your kids to remember that you're doing something different as a family.

GIVE THEM GRACE

If your kids are hungry and struggling to keep their fast—stop right there and pray with them that God would satisfy their hunger. If they need to eat, give them grace and let them eat. Remember, you don't want them to forfeit a lifelong discipline because of a legalistic experience when they are young.

CELEBRATE TOGETHER

Take time to share the joys of what God is doing in your life as a family. Celebrating where God is at work is a wonderful reward and motivator for kids who are learning to fast.

FASTING WITH YOUR CHURCH

How to Lead Your Church Through a Season of Fasting

F asting with your church has the potential to be a life-changing experience for everyone involved. But if you don't lead with humility and wisdom, then it can actually have the opposite effect. Although we still have a lot to learn, over the years we have learned some valuable lessons that have helped us experience some incredible fruit from our church with times of prayer and fasting.

One of the biggest takeaways from our journey thus far is that if you want to lead your church through a meaningful season of prayer and fasting, there are three distinct seasons—each with unique needs—through which you must lead your church.

SEASON 1: PREPARING BEFORE THE FAST

One of the questions I often get is, "How much time is needed to prepare a church properly for an extended time of prayer and fasting?" The answer to that question depends on two important realities:

How experienced is your church with the communal practice of fasting?

What is the duration of your church-wide fast?

I have found that the lower the level of experience and the longer the duration of the fast, the more time you need to prepare your church.

LEVEL OF EXPERIENCE + DURATION OF FAST = AMOUNT OF PREPARATION TIME

So for example, if you are calling your church to a short, one- or two-day communal fast, then the preparation time can be very short. You could deliver one sermon on the topic, give your church a helpful resource or two, and then call them to a day of prayer and fasting that week—probably with great success.

But if you plan to call people to an extended fast that will require more discipline and discomfort (at times) in every area of their lives, then the level of preparation will be more involved.

When our church is preparing for a month-long fast, we typically attempt to prepare them in the following ways (in this order):

1. We explain the **why**.
2. We explain the **what**.
3. We explain the **how**.

This book includes the basic premise of what we try to communicate regarding the why, the what, and the how, so you can use it as part of your preparation. Our church will distribute this book to each person in our church three weeks before the fast begins. That way, our church can think through each of these areas individually as we prepare to fast communally.

GETTING LEADERS ON BOARD

We always start by ensuring our leaders are "in." We want to make sure they understand why we think an extended season of prayer and fasting is needed and will be helpful. Next, we try to help them understand the practical implications of what we're calling them into (i.e., what kind of fast, for how long, etc.), and finally we work to clearly explain how we will function together as leaders during the fast. So for example, during our month-long fasts, we ask all of our leaders to come together for an hour of prayer and worship each day.

Once all our leaders are on board, we begin to prepare our church, typically three to four weeks before the fast begins. We use a variety of tools to help communicate the why, the what, and the how of prayer and fasting. In addition to what we discussed in Part 4 of this book, we do a few things to help our church prepare together:

- ✕ Our **Sunday Sermons** leading up to the fast are designed to **inspire** our people toward prayer and fasting, **inform** them of how to prepare for our time of prayer and fasting, and then **invite** them to practically take their next step with prayer and fasting.
- ✕ We provide **simple resources** (like this book), which are designed to help you address the practical questions surrounding prayer and fasting.
- ✕ We leverage online content such as **blogs** and **social media posts** to share wisdom from people within our church who have practical insight into prayer and fasting in relation to a variety of seasons of life (i.e., fasting as a parent with young kids, fasting if you have health issues, fasting if you are a nursing mother, etc.).
- ✕ We share inspiring and powerful **testimonies** of how God has touched our church family in past seasons of prayer and fasting.
- ✕ We **set the bar low** by encouraging people to take a small first step and then grow from there. During our month-long fasts, we give people permission to fast in a variety of ways (as described in Part 4). In our church, we work hard to celebrate all steps of obedience, not just the "big ones."

SEASON 2: DURING THE FAST

Once the fast has begun, there are a few ways we try to spur our church on toward deeper levels of intimacy with God and each other:

× We provide a **daily prayer guide** that helps our church pray together throughout the week, even though we don't always see each other face-to-face during the week.

× We provide **daily encouragement** through social media and email blasts to help people focus on the Word of God.

× We enlist people from our church to write **short blog posts detailing the ups and downs** of their experience of prayer and fasting. We share these with the church throughout the fast.

× As we did in the season of preparation, we provide space for a variety of **testimonies** (of both successes and struggles) each Sunday when we gather for worship.

× On Sundays, we create a lot of **space in our worship gatherings for corporate prayer**. When we first started fasting as a church, we were not accustomed to praying together corporately, so we would devote approximately eight to ten minutes each Sunday to guided, corporate prayer. As our prayer culture began to shift over the years, it's not uncommon for us to now spend thirty minutes or more in corporate prayer in our Sunday gatherings during the fast.

SEASON 3: CONCLUDING THE FAST

Over the last few years, we have discovered that how you prepare for the end of a fast is just as important as how you prepare for the start of a fast. We learned this lesson the hard way. The first time our church spent an extended season in prayer and fasting, we prepared them well on the front end, but completely neglected what it would be like to come out of that intense season on the back end.

We learned a simple lesson.

Seasons of spiritual **intensity** often force us to develop new levels of **intentionality** that nearly always lead to increased **intimacy**.

INTENSITY + INTENTIONALITY = INTIMACY

That first year, we discovered that our preparation before the fast and our time together during the fast produced a level of spiritual intensity we had not anticipated. For the record, this was a very good thing! This level of intensity led many of our people toward a much greater level of intentionality during the fast. People really worked hard to rearrange their priorities around the Lord. Our church sought the heart of God together in some really incredible ways during that first season of fasting, and it was awesome.

But the pace for many of our people was simply unsustainable. So when they got to the end of the fast, many felt a sense of spiritual whiplash. For an entire month, they had been stretched like a spiritual rubber band to the very edge of their capacity, and then suddenly the rubber band was released and snapped back way further than they anticipated.

Many felt a sense of spiritual whiplash

For many, when the **intensity** went away, so did the **intentionality** and eventually the **intimacy**.

But by the grace of God, we learned some great lessons, and what doesn't kill you makes you stronger. In the years since, we have begun to really think about how we help our people enter into their "new normal" after a season of prayer and fasting. After all, we don't want them to go back to where they were before the fast but to keep stepping forward into the future with God.

Last year, just as we took three weeks to prepare for the fast, we took three weeks on the back end to process the fast. That may sound excessive, but it was absolutely incredible. Here's how it worked:

- ✕ On the **last Sunday of the fast**, we helped our people take note of all that God had done in them personally during the fast, and then communally we gave thanks to God.
- ✕ On the **first Sunday after the fast**, we helped our people discern personally what spiritual rhythms from the fast they needed to **hold on to** (i.e., daily prayer with their family, focused time in the Word, etc.) and what things they needed to continue to **let go of** or engage

differently (i.e., many reduced their time watching TV, using social media, etc.) now that the fast was over.

× On the **second Sunday after the fast**, we concluded our time of processing by clearly identifying next steps for our communal pursuit of God.

This strategic approach on the back end of our extended seasons of prayer and fasting has helped us keep the **intentionality** and the **intimacy** even when the level of **intensity** shifts.

LEAD WELL ... YOUR WAY

The above suggestions are not a formula, merely a framework. My hope is that you would take some of these suggestions and adjust them appropriately to fit your context. I also hope you will discern which ideas won't work for your church. Better yet, I hope you will discover new ways of leading your church family into meaningful seasons of prayer and fasting, and then one day, I pray you will share them with us. Regardless of what it looks like, I hope that you will lead your people into the full-throttled pursuit of God with courage and clarity.

ABOUT THE AUTHOR

DAVE CLAYTON is a follower of Jesus, husband to Sydney, and dad to Micah, Jack, and Judah. He lives in Nashville, Tennessee, where he helps lead Ethos Church, Onward Church Planting, and Awaken Nashville. Dave is passionate about making disciples, planting churches, and awakening a movement for the glory of God, the joy of the church, and the good of the multitudes who don't yet know Jesus.